LEARNING TOGETHER

LEARNING TOGETHER

AVERY NIGHTINGALE

CONTENTS

CHAPTER 1

Introduction

In this chapter, we provide an overview of what we learned about relationship development during the intergenerational learning experiences that caregivers and children, as well as older adults, adults, and college students, shared. We describe how college students and community-based learning (CBL) experiences are situated in the directionality of fostering membership in the intergenerational community setting. We present observations of the learning process as well as the measurable learning outcomes for students, in terms of both being readied for their futures and for the opportunity to observe the returns on their commitment to community. We describe the role of the interconnected individuals, institutions, and communities in the establishment and maintenance of powerful learning experiences, providing both societal and individual benefits.

As students and teachers from diverse backgrounds participate in high-quality, high-reciprocity learning experiences, a number of facilitators can enhance the learning and relationship-building process. Many skills needed for effective practice and assimilation of new information and experiences emanate from the abilities of highly skilled teachers. In this case, students were challenged with new learning; when the outcomes also were new or different from usual experiences, apprehension increased. Students' concerns about whether they would be accepted as "reasonably capable" by organizational partners were somewhat reduced, however, by the orientation experience during community service learning.

CHAPTER 2

The Importance of Building Relationships in Educat

Educators in schools and colleges create meaningful educational experiences for students through a mix of personal and professional interactions. Many students – for good or for ill – choose to engage in particular courses and educational experiences because of relationships they have built with educators who teach in those programs. Undergraduate students often identify making connections with faculty as one of the most important things they can do during their undergraduate experience, and graduate students frequently cite their advisor as a key person in their success and satisfaction in their programs. It is the relationship we have with students that gives us the opportunity to help, lead, encourage, and support them as we work together to create successful educational experiences.

At a recent college parent orientation, we talked extensively about our philosophy of care. Our platform includes tips on how to make a good first impression, how to build positive relationships that foster cooperation, how to communicate in ways that encourage students, and how and when to refer students to appropriate support services. But what is really important in our approach is summarized in a common phrase, "Caring is not enough." It takes caring plus something – in this case, our expertise as educators – to make the most of the relationships we develop with students.

CHAPTER 3

Creating a Positive Learning Environment

Educational experiences are shared experiences, learning experiences are social experiences, and, for that reason, social and emotional safety is of utmost importance. If I come into the room feeling shrieked, that will affect my ability to learn. Thus, I spend the vast majority of the first days of school cultivating a classroom culture of trusting relationships, a united unit of learners. I utilize a combination of class building activities with physical games to teach and establish respect and cooperation. Modeling how to be inclusive, especially when we are discouraged from doing so, is imperative. Right from the beginning, I make my expectations clear to my students: "In our classroom, everyone belongs; everyone's voice is important, and your ideas and contributions will be respected."

Both the physical and emotional environments need to be conducive to laughter and conversation throughout every learning experience. Part of the human experience is not only the ability to learn from others, but, more importantly, to learn with others. Reciprocal relationships are critical to any educational setting, adult or child, and are the foundation of building trusting, respectful relationships between students and educators. By creating these positive relationships, we become more entitled in the learning process, and, as a result, the classroom culture becomes a united unit. I borrow cultures as we are all the sum of the multiple cultures that define and create our experiences. Thus, the learning environment is impacted by and impacts all its participants. In this chapter, I explore creating a culture of care in which all students authentically access and engage in learning experiences that support unlimited possibilities both inside and beyond the classroom walls.

CHAPTER 4

Collaborative Learning Strategies

On the heart-to-heart relationships, the authors noted the importance of receiving feedback and building from it in genuine ways; there must be a concerted effort to create and maintain a genuine quality from the interactions in our shared learning environments. One of the strategies is known as an Individual/Class Tactan Project. Everyone is a teacher, learner, facilitator, and student. Sicko and Buschler mentioned that when combined with the necessary rigor, heart-to-heart sharing interactions lead to flourishing learning ecologies. Connecting our personal experiences to professional or class experiences, according to Bransford, Brown, and Cocking, provide structures for successful learning. Moreover, lavender/other plant-like objects have been shown to lower blood pressure readings and connect personal learning experiences to professional successes (less sick days from school for children) and class (better retention of the

9/11 information and role of formal structures for knowledge construction in children ages 3-6).

Hokanson and Hooper in their video presentation mentioned that the authors had tested many different strategies in the classroom and for a variety of audiences outside of the classroom. Based on their exhaustive testing of strategies, the authors concluded that genuine care for authentic understanding must be shown to all individuals and that truly effective strategies for the classroom ensure that "inner relationships" of experience come to the forefront of learning experiences. Individually-led projects are treated like distributed ethics and finally collective sharing units are formed as a way of distributing the outcome of the projects to the inner relationships through our design requests. The authors believe that these relationships and strategies for them help to form "people-to-people" and "heart-to-heart" relationships within the learning environment.

CHAPTER 5

Using Technology to Enhance Educational Experience

Integrating technology is not without challenges. As a society that evolves alongside technology, it is important to ensure safe and secure experiences. Trust and rapport are important in face-to-face relationships, and trust in technology used in the learning environment must be maintained. As with any complex project, safety and security concerns take first priority. It is also important to allow students opportunities to create relationships and develop physical interactions outside of those mediated by technology, regardless of the given situation. Current events may force isolation, but evolution should be part of any successful life. With all realistic concerns, we have opportunities for growth and learning. By using educational technology to facilitate academic growth and relationship building, barriers are addressed and then broken.

Technology offers powerful solutions to overcome physical distance and time limitations. The ability to utilize technology as part of the curriculum creates opportunities that may not have been available otherwise. By providing integrated educational experiences that bring together students from multiple learning environments, lines of communication are opened, thus bridging opportunity gaps. Many educational platforms have integrated communication tools available to allow meaningful learning experiences to take place. Throughout the school year, teachers and students can join classes from multiple schools to learn alongside and from one another. Students can work together to facilitate science experiments, perform dissections, or share cultural experiences with peers whom they otherwise would never have had a relationship. This ability to bridge learning barriers helps implement and demonstrate relationship bridges between students and teachers to further build the learning community. By understanding that by working together, our potential is limitless, we are able to create learning opportunities that flourish through student experiences as well as with support from teachers, parents, and technology workers.

CHAPTER 6

Promoting Inclusivity and Diversity in Education

Ideally, a teacher will work with individual learners in designing educational experiences in a way that forwards long-term growth in knowledge, skills, and values for all learners, regardless of their differences. Future research should focus on measuring the effect of inclusive strategies on the learners; presumably using scores gained from modified designs of tasks; not whether a teacher used inclusive strategies.

It would be unreasonable to say that these inclusive-inspired strategies are either always necessary, practical, or implementable in classrooms. And it would also be unreasonable to say that not all teachers are currently addressing this growing challenge. For example, an aggressive position from a teacher or instructor to provide specially designed materials for each student, built around each student's worldview, which is inclusive in this example a single time, may actually undermine a student's overall long-term success. For example, a teacher catering specially to an individual student, taking excessive amounts of time designing a single activity or learning object, while the other learners are forgotten.

In our complex world, rather than being threatened by an unknown, education can be a place where new knowledge, new thoughts, and the background knowledge of cultures different from our own are embraced – creating a stronger, more capable society. For this to happen, we must take a more aggressive stance in promoting inclusivity and diversity within almost all educational interactions.

In our world today, culture and society are changing rapidly, with no sign of slowing. Many of those changes, especially technological, have ever-increasing impacts on our educational experiences. Teachers and instructional designers already have a tough job: to teach and support learning in an ever-changing society. Designing educational experiences that are never outdated takes substantial creativity and considerable patience. Furthermore, just as technology evolves, so does the demographics of our society. These demographic changes can lead to grouping students by social differences.

CHAPTER 7

Fostering Social and Emotional Learning

Social and personal skills or competencies involving students working with others must also be built. Communication, teamwork, leadership, conflict management, personal responsibility, global and inter-cultural effectiveness, and interpersonal relations are considered important competencies. It's important to learn to work together, to practice and learn from taking leadership roles, to foster others in leadership, dialogue with others, promote civil, effective and harmonious interaction and leadership, and to solve and understand a variety of difficult relationships. Emotional learning skills (SEL). The five essential social skills apply to the case of formal long-term mentoring programs and this chapter highlights five aspects: (1) self-awareness and self-management, (2) ability for social health and respectful behavior with other people (3) – positive relationship skills, rejecting substances (4) – decision making (5) impatient handling and patience. Social education. Recognize the connection between SEL and Mentorships.

Developmental tasks are often the focus of informal learning experiences. A key part of the college experience that you and your mentee may want to explore together, if you are both interested, is to help your mentee with developmental tasks. They include achieving independence, choosing and preparing for a career, and becoming an overall healthy adult. All of these tasks provide an opportunity for an educational experience from which everyone involved can benefit. One way of ensuring that your mentee becomes a successful student is to help him or her develop the appropriate study skills. Fundamental study skills—time management, note taking, reading, writing, listening, creativity, critical thinking, and test taking—are useful to all students. Learn the following to help your mentee develop these study skills: Ten Steps of Time Management, ideal practices for taking course notes, effective reading strategies, basics of written communication, how to listen critically, enhancing creativity, fostering critical thinking, and reducing test anxiety.

CHAPTER 8

Encouraging Active Student Engagement

In the learning setting, students who permit 'mental space' to reflect on subjective experiences may express engagement by revealing social, communicative, and metacognitive expressions 'in their minds.' Teachers can listen, paying attention to, inviting tune or validating these expressions, and/or returning responsibility and control over social interactions. It is paramount for teachers to understand the underlying regulatory network of relationships that sustains children's active engagement as well as its constitutive and influential impact on their shared psychological network central to school adjustments, success, and relationships. The goal is to highlight how small-group strategies connected to curricular content might promote active student engagement, ultimately assuring its sustainability across inclusive educational contexts. Teachers will understand how to listen, design social interactions and ultimately feel an increased level of understanding and empathy toward both typically developing and students who struggle.

One of the keys to ensuring active student engagement is for teachers to allow control over certain aspects of the learning. Students who perceive that they have choice in their interactions with the surroundings, the types of learning content, or the ways in which they engage in their education may feel more motivated and behave more responsibly. has described the 'transactional' nature of teaching that encourages growth in the social environment. Using circle-based strategies, I wished to screen for student choices. In building relationships, suggested that teachers "value spontaneity and intuition" and respond to their own students' unique individuality. Understanding that children also express themselves by small-group and partner conversational turns, the participants' natural responses seemed to reveal their emergent and active intentions. Each contained an expression of social, communicative, and/or metacognitive reflection and connection, or a combination thereof: some hinted evaluations of choices or preferences with an aim to influentially manage social exchanges, or sounded advances for collaborative and content learning goals.

CHAPTER 9

Developing Effective Communication Skills

This article describes two successive semesters of intensive training provided to early care and education undergraduate education and early childhood studies students to increase self-awareness and self-reflection relative to working with children with disabilities, and to increase the students' ability to communicate with the adults (parents or guardians) of these children. The training was part of a classroom-based project designed to provide students (39% of which were non-majors) enrolled in a two-semester sequence with intense valuable and pertinent experiences working with these children and the children's families. Interdisciplinary collaboration, hands-on practice, and exposure to additional strategies designed to involve young children with disabilities into typical educational environments have proven to be effective means of creating more positive attitudes and less apprehension for both caring for the children and sharing information about them with their parents and others.

Professionals are encouraged to develop and maintain open channels of communication with young children with disabilities. The unique developmental patterns and diverse needs of children with disabilities and their families pose challenges, particularly when communication breaks down. We examined undergraduate education and early childhood studies students' pre- and post-training ratings of self-efficacy and comfort levels in working with young children with a range of disabilities and their families, following a classroom intervention. The intervention was designed to expand students' ability to communicate with these important stakeholders. Results indicated some improvement from pre- to post-training in both self-efficacy and comfort levels, indicating increased feelings of confidence. However, students valued trainings particularly when they could interact directly with children with disabilities.

CHAPTER 10

Building Teacher-Student Relationships

The student with hearing loss is the one who has more difficulty in the educational system, especially when he progresses from the early years of elementary school, up to the end of elementary schooling. For the student who has a mild, moderate or higher hearing loss, all the professional support involved only came from the first year of life, when they started receiving the programming of the auditory prosthesis in the high complexity health and after the student went to or is directed to educational institutions that perform interventions, normally, educators and relatives are really aware that it is necessary to make decisions and they make use of the available Academic Support Services, as required by federal law in early childhood education.

In the previous chapter, we identified that interaction in a learning environment is key to removing the social element from the situation and increasing participation and success. In this chapter, we take a closer look at the relationships between teachers and students and how they are supported. We present and discuss the need for orientation of teachers, training, construction of bridges between the professional and the student, building a network between the professional, the student and their family, and strengthening the national system that supports Educational Inclusion. After presenting it, we take into account the fact that our discussion involves exchanging experiences and thus validating good practices found.

CHAPTER 11

Parent and Community Involvement in Education

The NCLB and Section 1118 definitions of educational opportunities and other Parent Education are discussed, and detailed efforts in the Allegheny-Clarion Valley School District designed to meet the requirements and exceed the need for parent involvement are described. As such, the methods may reflect a mission to touch every family on the educational experience of the child, respond to a variety of diverse needs families in an economically and geographically diverse area, and provide a variety of operational opportunities necessary to provide the incentives and resources needed to earn a report. Realistic initiatives that need to realize most significant involvement by the many partnerships involved.

The Initiative for the Education and Re-Education of Parents Committee, Vandergrift, a local affiliate of the Pennsylvania Association for Parent Involvement in Education, assembled a team of authors to identify learning opportunities and other parent education that meet the requirements of the governance in NCLB.

Parent and Community Involvement in Education. The federal No Child Left Behind (NCLB) Act of 2001, Public Law 107-110, requires many actions specifically to encourage and establish parent and community involvement in schools. Section 1118 describes a number of parental involvement initiatives that schools must, or at least should, take to maximize the learning potential of their students. Several of these initiatives include the provision of educational opportunities and other parent education needed to pursue these opportunities.

Assessing and Providing Feedback on Student Progre

To be effective, feedback should be timely, specific, and relevant. Furthermore, by involving peers in the feedback process, students can more easily give and receive feedback from others. In settings where students are encouraged to be active agents in their learning, enabling them to offer and accept feedback is particularly important as collaborative metacognitive practices foster deeper engagement which can lead to higher student achievement and a greater sense of competence.

Providing feedback that is specific, descriptive, and constructive is an important aspect of teaching and learning. By providing high-quality feedback, teachers help students to understand where they are in their learning, and what needs to be done to make further progress. Feedback can take many forms including written and/or verbal comments on written work, explanations teachers offer students on the results of a classroom assessment, and critiques teachers offer students on class discussions.

Formative assessments are used to collect data on student progress in relation to learning goals and can have a variety of purposes including to inform instruction, monitor student progress, and provide feedback. They include structured interactions that require students to explain and demonstrate their thinking, and performance tasks that require students to use what they have learned in authentic contexts.

Assessment involves collecting information about what students know and can do. This process provides valuable information for teachers and students and helps to guide instruction. When professionals work together to conduct assessments, they can learn from shared insights and work together to improve the learning experiences for all students.

CHAPTER 13

Supporting Students with Special Needs

We can help struggling students gain independence by teaching them to view their area of difficulty as a problem to be solved, which allows them to take more active responsibility for their own learning. For example, a student who has not been doing so well in school can be assigned the task of setting up a small focus group for the class. In this way, instead of experiencing himself as someone who has always been weak in school, he experiences himself as being both strong in conversation and as a nexus that contributes to the class. In the same way, a student who is seen as difficult in a social setting can be assigned the task of including students who are often excluded. By doing so, he becomes the link between students and the class community and can thus begin to explore an alternative to the role he is used to.

We learn more when we have to explain something we have learned to someone else. If we work with a range of students, we use our minds more frequently than if we only work with students with whom we have plenty in common. Clearly, the small groups of students in schools are filter bubbles, but we can use this situation to our advantage. For example, the principle of the group explication also applies to groups of teachers. Students with special needs, who are educated in inclusive settings, experience three times the amount of spoken language in schools, which indicates that teacher presence and teaching is more intensive than if the students are placed in special needs schools.

CHAPTER 14

Cultivating a Growth Mindset in Education

Yet to build growth mindsets in our students, we need to challenge ourselves. This is not about curriculum or rigor or scaffolding or support or wonder. This is about how we perceive our students, their potential, and our role as educators. We must be challenged to find the value in things that adults no longer find spark joy. We must be challenged to see the value of failure, not just as a learning tool, but a way to build emotional resilience in our students as they encounter past choices, life circumstances, and people who will support or challenge them. We must be challenged to engage in the passion of lifelong learning to strive for our own growth and model the risk-taking we state is essential for our students. We must be challenged to "do school" in a way that does not take the time at school for granted, and does not believe that age-based differentiation is the only way to have effective educational experiences.

It probably will not surprise you to learn that my best college professor was a high school teacher. Steve Cohen has taught in the Whitesboro Central School District, just outside Utica, New York, for over two decades. My love of teaching inspired me to think not only of Steve's influence on me, but my role as a teacher and my influence on my students. I realized I wanted to do more. Eleanor Roosevelt once said, "No one can make you feel inferior without your consent." I always have discussions with my students about what that statement meant to them, but in recent years I have added, "Even you cannot make you feel inferior if you don't let you." More and more I find myself speaking with college students about the idea of a "Growth Mindset". This idea, formulated by Carol Dweck from Stanford University, is the belief that intelligence, creativity, and technical skills are not set and unchanging - not something we have, but rather something we achieve. You are not smart, but rather you have learned and grown.

CHAPTER 15

Enhancing Critical Thinking and Problem-Solving Sk

Socrates's line "I cannot teach anybody anything, I can only make them think" might be absolutely true today. Although Socrates promoted acquiring knowledge, he was convinced that an unexamined life was not worth living, and the development of investigative thinking was the most valuable skill. He upheld methods like thinking aloud, asking questions, or guiding someone to arrive at a self-discovered truth as he realized that true learning and achievement can be accomplished only when knowledge is acquired through critical reasoning and investigation, rather than from ready-made facts. Today, knowledge is at everyone's fingertips. What could be the natural evolution of education concepts in the personalized and digital age? Fredrik Reinfeldt, the prime minister of Sweden, believes that the key to developing 21st-century skills is open and social learning, and that the integration of social components into online courses is the best of two worlds.

While technical skills are important for the workforce, employers maintain that critical thinking and problem-solving skills are the most critical for success. When was the last time a teacher was hired for being smart without having the ability to think critically or solve problems? The purpose of education is to pass knowledge, but the true essence is to develop skills for growth and progress. What happened to the teaching of these skills? Have some of the global education innovators been wrong and off the mark in preferring the teaching of 21st-century skills? An analysis of personal and professional failures, less than optimal decisions, and the Fukushima earthquake reveals that substantial progress on complex challenges can be achieved through the application of the age-old critical thinking and problem-solving skills, especially when these are consistently and systematically cultivated. Thanks to globalization, everyone has access to the same knowledge. The differences among individuals will be significant when they depend mostly on skills.

CHAPTER 16

Integrating Arts and Creativity in Education

For most children, the best lessons seem to be the ones where they are privileged to participate, are engaged, and directly involved. The academic community has always recognized that students are able to learn according to their intellectual, cultural, emotional, and physical experiences or what is generally referred to as their multiple modes of perception. New information will be selectively preferred by students in different ways. Obligating students to determine the most beneficial path to learning over time will encourage and increase the chance for meaningful learning to occur. The United States government and governments throughout the world have increasingly emphasized the requirement for training in science, mathematics, technology, and engineering (STEM) subjects. The Carolina University Challenge to "Think and Do" and the Voices of Change at UNCG require the visual, musical, and dramatic arts to develop advanced creativity, a fundamental component of learning in the 21st century. In a recent study, multidisciplinary art programs proved to be particularly valuable in the learning of students. In these analyses, children chose multi-topic creative training instead of single discipline training: they were able to share their intellectual abilities without feeling sluggish by something specific or showing promise from superior performing arts. In the same study, the visual arts students successfully examined, interpreted, and tried knowledge.

Integrated arts practice in teaching and learning creates an atmosphere ripe for innovative possibilities, opening up the potential of what may be accomplished. It is commonly defined as the interconnection of at least two artistic disciplines (such as visual art, music, drama, and dance). The integration of arts performance is where learning is tangible, visible, and experiences are created. However, the arts expression and expertise of children trained in the arts promotes verbal, emotional, and expressive intelligence that can serve to advantage other forms of learning. Individually and collectively, specific art forms inspire and foster creativity within the participants. By its nature, integrated arts align with brain functions, inspiring the rational and creative processes. By involving the frontal lobe, the process allows for higher function thinking. In the creations of a melded work of display, all avenues toward solving problems are evident. It is this form of education or integration that gives rise to creativity. Creativity differs from intelligence in that it is not focused on how much abnormal data will be retained. Using different aspects of the brain, creativity allows for making novel presentations that share uniqueness and value.

CHAPTER 17

Promoting Global Citizenship Education

It is necessary to understand what we are facing. In the modern world, affected by formidable terrorists and intimidating warmongering, 'a more balanced civil society' does not make the briefings fast enough, and this way is very much alive. It also lacks diplomats who work to resolve problems before they become crises. Global citizenship needs to promote social and political anything else but the sixth revtech revolution of civilization – and many associated with it are unwise. A World at School offers much groundless, largely because they blindly take "progress" and "inevitably" on faith and convert them into sort of a new religion. But how can we serve a higher good if we lack a wise, meaningful, and honest foundation for our search? How can we argue those principles, especially when the embracing of inevitable "innovations," such as self-driving cars, causes partially prove that "the expanding spiral of scientific and technological advancements" does not translate into socially responsible behavior, in particular care of our endangered environment?

Unlike a magazine essayist who accumulates facts and opinions on a late-breaking issue through web search, cutting and pasting them together into one piece, citing sources that have not been read, I am not presenting an article of that type wherein explicit citation and what I am suggesting is not information warfare tenets (that is, tactical/official introduces conflicting information, disinformation, and strange narratives about real events into the information space, and social activists respond not in kind but by presenting true information in the form of the message), line of operation.

This paper is designed to raise awareness of targeted efforts to educate children and young people about current global issues and the reasoning behind them in the struggling world of our global civilization, which faces future impoverishment of the environment and water resources, societal collapse, financial crash, and many other issues. By exploring the current philosophies that form global citizenship education, my aim here is to assist people in finding and justifying a socially, environmentally, and economically sustainable sense of global citizenship, as well as values that underpin sustainable behavior, emotions, cultural conceptions, and planetary connection.

CHAPTER 18

Addressing Bullying and Promoting Kindness

Research has shown that young children recognize the impor-tance of kindness, and they will, conversely, judge unkindness as be-havior that is hurtful (Popovic, 2014). Therefore, to promote kind actions and be helpers in the classroom/school and other areas of their lives, children and youth need opportunities for social and emotional learning. They should receive age-appropriate informa-tion, get help in reflecting on their actions and how others are feel-ing, as well as what they can do to help in the event of another person experiencing unkind behavior or some other challenges. It is common knowledge that children learn through their own ex-periences. Therefore, it is important to offer them opportunities for these observations and experiences through various activities, in-cluding storytelling and art. On various websites, we can find sev-eral proposals regarding workshops and activities through which children and youth can encourage creative and emotional thinking;

enable the development of imaginative abilities; participate in the cultural exchange; contribute to the development of understanding and empathy, while contributing to building relationships with others and encourage them to act kindly, as well as creating communities of social change.

Bullying is a term that is widely explored, and many tend to think that they have a good understanding and concept of what is bullying. The phenomenon of bullying is often recognized as present in schools and workplaces, but it can also appear in other contexts. As a concept, bullying consists of two basic components: aggression and power imbalance. According to Wasti and coworkers (2019), bullying can be defined as "negative behaviors towards a victim, displayed frequently and persistently, by the use of a variety of tools or methods, and often including elements of humiliation and abuse of power, which adversely affect the victim (p.1)." Despite these elements being generally accepted, it is notable that those who study such phenomena (including children and youth) have different understandings and categorization, or at least, it can be argued that their views are affected by their own experiences, understandings, definitions, and cultural differences.

Implementing Project-Based Learning Approaches

It is then through these designing educational movements that the aspirations of the marginalized, including learning experienced by prisoners, can be furthered. Just as every individual in Gaza is a vibrant being, so also are they deliberate teachers of their lives. With more than fifty-three percent of the population under eighteen years, children in the Strip are paying not only the human cost of conflict but also the psychological, emotional, and educational impact of the lack of political recognition within the larger discourse of development. Juxtaposed with the approximate forty-six percent of people living under the poverty line and approximately six percent of women being part of higher education, with the mass cultural constraints, it becomes not only policy intervention but also a sheer symbol of hope retained by them.

In the tight infrastructure of the Gaza Strip, a constant influx of persons and materials can create an overwhelming feeling. Situated densely in a narrow strip, due to a historical blockade imposed by the Israeli government, not much changes in Gaza. Even with rumblings of political unrest, commercial industries or progress, the typical imagery of Palestine overshadows the Gazan splendors often disregarded. But amidst the chaos and congestion emerges something beautiful – laughter. Innocent grins can breathe renewed hope through homes made of rubble and an inculcated resilience that a caged animal develops. This is the essence of humanity that educators can nurture and teach, helping to provide children experiences directing their own education.

CHAPTER 20

Encouraging Independent Learning and Self-Reflecti

Model: You can demonstrate this by discussing issues available at the table, thinking aloud or "thinking and solving out loud". Teachers adapt their own cognitive processes to think aloud so students can understand how problems are interpreted, discussed, devised, and solved. A simplified version of think-aloud can be seen and learned by younger students. This helps to break complex learning problems into a series of small problems and use dedicated problem-solving skills and strategies. A computer scientist should think and solve during everyday lecture tasks. Show students your willingness to take chances; it's okay not to know all the answers. At times, it may be helpful to share personal struggles and, together, explore solutions to problems in situations that are difficult to solve. When this occurs, teachers need to balance tolerance, compassion, and help, without enabling or overwhelming the student. Thoughtfulness is something that is nurtured and specific, and although students are given the necessary resources, they can be challenged and encouraged to assume independence of thought.

In this chapter, we will learn strategies for fostering a classroom environment of independent learning and self-reflection. As educators, we have a critical role in empowering students to work autonomously, think critically, and develop the necessary skills to synthesize information and facts. We encourage our students to think through the steps of problem solving, put personal effort into their work, and self-assess the quality of their understanding. Their work is also a personal reflection on their part, as they think about what they learned, what was well-understood, and what weaknesses were discovered. Here are some ways that educators might establish a more self-reliant culture in the classroom.

CHAPTER 21

Using Experiential Learning to Deepen Understandin

Experiential learning enables participants in the process of building relationships, as stated "across physical and digital space". Similarly found that by using an activity theory framework, their observation of cognitive load could be applied not just to individual learning, but to more complex interactions in a digital gaming setting. The relationships and interactions that experiential learning can build can transcend the application settings that most information literacy courses are constrained by, enabling successful outcomes in distance and online educational experiences, as well as face-to-face ones. In their study of the use of media tablets in undergraduate classroom projects, found that experiential learning provided not just encouragement for new participatory models; it also allowed for richer experiences than the traditional textual submissions found within traditional courses, thus benefiting both the students and their future instructors.

Experiential learning allows learners to deepen their own understanding of the material being presented, often allowing them to receive proactive feedback. This provides ample opportunities for participants to reflect on their own shifting paradigms as they seek to interpret the world through reflective observation and abstract conceptualization. This process ties in with deepening of learning in an educational context, which in turn prepares learners for postgraduate or professional pathways. The information literate person recognizes that while they will never be defined as a full expert in their research area, they are continuously expanding their skill set to what presents as the emerging level of expertise - the journey.

CHAPTER 22

Incorporating Outdoor and Environmental Education

Just going backpacking or participating in a trek in the wilderness obviously has value on many levels. People on such experiences may be with friends, family, or other groups in a truly unique outdoor setting without the phones and normal electronic devices that most people are connected with on a day-to-day basis. If a deeper and perhaps greater level of potential outcomes is desired with well-suited individuals, it might be wise to look a little deeper into the reasons for taking them outside in the first place. Positive outdoor experiences result whether it is sunny with no rain or snow, whether everyone is a comfortable temperature and dry, whether meal preparation is stress-free and all of the correct dishware and utensils acquired before leaving, and so on. It is possible to design an outdoor and environmental education experience that provides many benefits to the individuals involved. With substantial planning, preparation, collaboration, cooperation among and between diverse professions, and broad community awareness, the levels of outcomes may be far greater. With notable, carefully planned, and overlapping educational experiences (outside, inside, together), the connections within the systems, of which Earth is a part, are likely to be enhanced.

Simply going outside with a group can be an enjoyable experience. While well-planned backpacking trips, outdoor adventures, and nature experiences give all individuals value, creating the plan, thinking in advance about the objectives, goals, time frame, stage of group development, and activities offered greatly enhances a positive experience and ultimate outcomes. A critical aspect of outdoor and environmental education is having an objective. From the many great program options such as multi-day backpacking trips, day hikes, leadership and teambuilding exercises, ropes courses, nature walks and studies, formal environmental education projects, and challenging team problem-solving opportunities, an instructor or facilitator can provide a positive experience for the participants.

CHAPTER 23

Building Resilience and Grit in Students

Some of our best teachers are bringing their students through obstacles and challenges. More public school teachers are setting up their rooms as personal learning environments and facilitating projects. These teachers are keeping themselves connected to students. Having strong relationships will make changes in teacher practices less frightening for our teachers and increase student motivation. We should direct a balanced approach in describing students' work and attitudes. We should always give our sincere interests and enthusiasm. What we are really interested in, and should emphasize when we communicate with students, is learning. We should always ask questions about learning and what was done for learning. It's only natural for students to be proud of the quest for knowledge. We all are. But giving them praise for doing what is expected in a classroom is not the support for developing resilience or grit.

The school year is coming to a close. Summer is almost here. This, of course, is an exciting time. There are year-end field trips, barbecues, and it is the season of year-end pool parties and graduations. These celebrations are a fun way to formally and informally mark the end of another school year. High school, college, and elementary school graduates do not always realize the emotional meaning of these transitions. It is a time to consider all that the students learned during the year, and how they experienced it with all their many successes and failures. They may also need to consider the future and if they are ready. Are we making our students resilient or are we offering well-intentioned but misguided praise that keeps them from developing necessary qualities such as autonomy, grit, and resilience?

CHAPTER 24

Supporting Teacher Professional Development

As the session ended, participants began to exit the room, despite Zis' announcement that there were almost 30 minutes left of class. Zis asked everyone to sit back down and tell the person seated next to them something they appreciated about them as a future colleague. Finally, the instructors had to call the class to an official end, as time had run out. The student teachers left the room with smiles on their faces. Researchers have explored the power of each of these strategies to develop teachers who will advocate for high-quality practices while actively participating in respectful relationships. Additionally, many teacher educators create potential for future collegial support systems through co-constructing courses with teacher candidates in innovative, inclusive, relationship-building ways.

This implemented one of her professional development projects for student teachers. As project facilitator, her goal was to create a safe, inviting space in which student teachers could discuss anti-bias education, supporting their growth toward effective, responsive practitioners. One of the students who had just begun speaking said, "I know my voice is shaking. This is something I feel really emotional about... This is something that I'm nervous about teaching to my students, but I know that I have to." The student's genuine emotion touched everyone, and for the remainder of the session, the group engaged in a meaningful discussion about how to engage students in conversations about racial differences and inequality.

CHAPTER 25

Nurturing a Love for Lifelong Learning

In the Primary years Programme of the International Baccalaureate curriculum, students are actively engaged, and asked to "tune into" themselves: reflect on opinions, build knowledge of the world, and work to know oneself. Further, inquiry-based learning is fostered. Assuring appropriate age, physical, cognitive, and emotional development for our youngest students builds confidence in learners. Holistically, nurturing and developing the Primary years Programme learner profile attributes through positive learning environments leads to helping create students who are able to grow in stages cognitively and emotionally while exhibiting the traits needed to be future ministers to the greater good of society.

Studies show that by age four, children with limited vocabularies tend to remain poor readers throughout school years. It is also pertinent to note that adolescent brain structure and development can be influenced by positive adult interaction. As educators, we have a moral and ethical responsibility to provide an environment that nurtures childhood growth and development so that our students come to full adulthood confident, well-rounded individuals.

Beginning Winsette School, my prayer for my students is that they come away from Winsette School with a love for lifelong learning. Development is an orderly, sequential process. A child cannot talk before he walks; he cannot read before recognizing shapes and having a basic vocabulary.

The Amish are a people who live simple, modest lives. One seldom hears of an Amish child who is regularly in trouble with the law, and the Amish test above average on intelligence tests. The heart of any school system is teacher-student interaction. The Amish put their arms around every student and draw them close. This type of nurturing love and interaction with teachers who are genuinely concerned for them as individuals makes learning a positive, fulfilling experience.

CHAPTER 26

Empowering Student Voice and Agency

Student-driven learning experiences provide learners with the opportunity to pursue passions, ask authentic questions, and solve problems that impact the community. By taking action to change a situation, students begin to take empathy into meaningful action by impacting the community in a positive way. This process makes the learning experience relevant and lasting. Instead of checking a box and continuing the cycle of experiences described above, we facilitate authentic conversation that puts students in conjunction with those their class serves as they move through the design thinking process. The "why" of learning becomes more important than the "what" because it builds connections to the world in which students learn, rather than those they will move on to. In recognizing this shift, methods of assessment that focus on student understanding and improvements through the learning process, rather than content memorization and regurgitation, are needed to provide value to the learner. Assessments such as reflective journals, digital port-folios, and presentations via paper slides give students the opportunity to connect learning to experiences and provide others with the opportunity to learn from and with how the student was able to impact the community during the design. These methods also reinforce the self-directed, motivated, and empathetic individuals we want our students to become.

As educators, our goal is to create learners, not just learners of school, but lifelong learners who are not confined to a school building or a school day. The way students learn is changing. Students and teachers are moving beyond the four walls of a classroom to explore the world, foster relationships, and build understanding through experiences. Education is transforming from content experts to experience architects who are able to empower the learners. Our students have literally called us out, and the responsibility inherent in this situation requires educators to create conditions where learners are making choices, building understanding with empathy, while pushing past limitations placed on student voice and agency. Teachers and schools have begun the shift to pedagogies that are impacting student outcomes by providing opportunities for students to learn in ways that are not confined to a school building or a limited number of hours. The learner is placed at the center of the learning experience, with teaching coaches operating in facilitating and guiding roles.

CHAPTER 27

Strengthening School-Home Partnerships

According to a NEA report, "positive school community rela-tionships such as those between students and teachers and students and their peers are essential to learning." It also cites research show-ing the benefits of school-home partnerships, which include better student grades, better student behavior, the adoption of effective teaching strategies in order to build and maintain rapport, and ad-vocates that (1) teachers create a learning environment where indi-viduals of diverse identity—i.e. race, color, national origin, language, ability, religion, socio-economic status, or sexual orientation—are respected as individuals, valued as members of their cultural iden-tities, and experience themselves as contributing members of the school community. (2) evidence-based practice that locates or creates meaningful relationships, understandings, and connection between and among students, parents and school, and; lastly, (3) the integration of neurological, psychological, sociological, educational, and leadership theories and practices.

Children learn not only from what they're taught but also from what they see around them. That means teachers and parents, as well as students and classmates, can take away lessons of their own from their interactions with one another. Ideally, schools support children educationally as well as emotionally, nurturing both their intellectual curiosity and their need for stability and security. But imagine if they nurtured their grown-ups, too. That is the core of the Academically & Socially Integrated Model (ASIM), a theoretical value model grounded in extensive educational philosophy and impactful activities that foster meaningful relationships and deepened understanding among parents, educators, and students. ASIM ultimately aims to cultivate strong reciprocal partnerships and generate transformational experiences at school and at home—both of which are critical to student success. The model, which harnesses collective impact leadership, is meant to be carried out through the use of our learning environments—be they classrooms, community spaces, or mobile apps—so that research can become action to inform policy and in practice.

CHAPTER 28

Promoting Health and Well-being in Education

Data from multiple studies reveal that education as a social system has a direct effect on the public health of our nation in terms of the well-being of students and staff. School health has also been used to frame specific prevention efforts of the Center for Disease Control. Within the application of PBIS, these negative outcomes are referred to as problem behavior ("to address socially significant problems," Dunlap & Fox, 1999). When it is said that problem behavior (at the school level) is prevented and not extinguished, the focus is on treating not only the outcome behavior but also the school practice that is promoting the behavior. In the same way that education environments need to build proficiency in reading, math, and science for all students across multiple contexts, education environments need to build proficiency in communication, social skills, self-awareness, and problem-solving skills across school settings, for all students.

This paper describes the Tier 1 interventions of the Michigan Student Data System Positive Behavioral Interventions and Supports Project (MiSIP). Specifically, MiSIP focuses on building educational experiences that are positive, predictable, safe, and nurturing in order to support all students across school settings. In particular, the current paper focuses on the first two components: school-wide expectations and routines and transitions. Tier 1 interventions are those that are put into place for all students across all settings using a systems approach and are more formally classified as universal supports. The Michigan State Board Policy and common practice outline this kind of universal programming for all students. In the same way that educational programming takes place with the goal of meeting the needs of all students, the goal of universal Tier 1 PBIS interventions is to promote an environment in which the diverse population of students in the public school system are provided with the clear, predictable, and consistent experiences that are needed to support behavioral and educational success. This is consistent with the intent of Policy 2410, Positive Behavioral Interventions and Supports (State Board of Education, 2006, 2011).

CHAPTER 29

Advancing STEM Education

By developing a program, which ranged from specifically designed hands-on activities to more complex forms of integrated action, the IIS used quality science learning models. A program structured bottom-up to emphasize the individual needs of the participants. Each course provided a basic tool, review lecture, and individual render. The Break Through Engineering alternative created a clear vocational progression. We made proposals and made clear what it takes for each step to be taken. For those previously involved in informal settings, teachers were given the most chance to join the program with their students. In response, the IIS's ability to work and learn from enrolling, with its powerful platforms for feedback and feedback. Over the university campus, what were the links and guidance involved in The Busy School of our Research involved in the special program.

After decades of pre-season cognitive and experiential learning opportunities, FIRST has emerged as a prime example of informal, year-round educational activity. Whether youth are involved in FIRST annually or during their school years, the environment created by FIRST marks an unprecedented opportunity for research. This paper characterizes this year-round learning environment, summarizes four years of data collection, and explores the research questions these data raise. To explore a year-round focus on hands-on learning, the paper summarizes challenges, including research agendas to be pursued and constraints placed on the work by the organization and its diverse community.

CHAPTER 30

Exploring Career and Vocational Education

Over the past three decades, educators have experienced numerous and ongoing reforms and trends in career and vocational education as the nation sought to update and improve educational opportunities for students. It was a time that began (early 1990s) with technology in the forefront, creating educational opportunities unique in teaching and learning. The early years that brought us the Internet and the development of web-based classes set a high-tech vision for the future. The world was changing at an accelerated rate as electronic information was accessed by using new technologies. Though the electronic classroom was neither new nor as successful as advocates suspected, the partnership of technology and education was transformative by providing a full array of communication opportunities connected to a rapidly expanding educational infrastructure.

It is a rare occurrence that the three of us who share our educational insights in these chapters are together for an extended period. Most often, we are spread out around the conference tables in our respective colleges or out looking for specific ways to engage our students while convincing politicians that what we do is an essential component of a comprehensive education. In part, this reflective career growth process with its embedded collegial discussions has been a way of compensating for our differing and sometimes overly segregated collegiate instruction and disciplinary demands. Our focus on self-reflective practices of educational development has allowed us to continue our personal and professional relationships unburdened by geographical restraints.

CHAPTER 31

Adapting to Remote and Online Learning Environment

Finally, another major drawback of this challenge is the unequal access to resources and supports students are experiencing and the toll it takes on their teachers. During the wrap-up discussion on the third day, one of the teachers expressed, "On top of dealing with everything being said... I really feel all the kids who basically have, you know, who have nothing. They come to school for lunch, you know. I worry about how they're going to be able to learn." The emotional burden and concern teachers have on the lives of their students cause great caution, stress, and anxiety. While students' learning struggles are with the expectations remote learning tools set, it is essential to acknowledge the struggles of their teachers and the personal, emotional, and academic burdens they carry with great care and perseverance in alignment with students' choices. Considering the experience of teachers as key collaborators in education settings and honing in on their testimonies using "what works for those who are doing it" frameworks helps bring their experiences to light to help inform student support systems in educational technology training.

As discussed earlier, the experiences of teaching remotely are all about struggle, less engagement, family engagement, and unequal access to supports. We also heard from other participants who have similar experiences to other studies' findings on the impact of the lack of supports from professionals and resources on students. Not having the level of professional support from professionals that are available in-class settings is causing a lot of emotional distress to teachers. Teachers in this study cared a lot about their students, and when they're not worried about their students' emotional distress, they were frustrated at the amount of energy they had to devote to get them to turn in their assignments and to get them to turn on their computers, and for some of them not even hearing from them at all.

CHAPTER 32

Conclusion

Educational experiences are not unique to HEIs as individuals can learn about something of interest or importance from their family members, friends, books, attending workshops, and then use both failures and successes to evolve their learning understanding. The expanded understanding of education as used in this presentation highlights the complexity and importance of a variety of individual perspectives. This extended definition is for the purpose of arguing that until one understands a phenomenon and its associated interpersonal relationships, one risks relying on misguided assumptions, quick judgments or selective conceptual history, which could further hamper our ability to construct effective and sustainable policies for improving the educational spaces that we share within our society.

Education is a representation of relationships both between individuals and within society. Additionally, the type of education received, including how, by whom and even where, is also a result of those relationships. Within the chapter, education is highlighted as an experience, where people serve as educational resources for each other. The education temporarily causes a group of people to work together through shared learning experiences. Both positive and negative relationships are formed when people work and engage within these shared learning experiences. Much of the education within this chapter occurs in higher education institutions (HEIs) but can also encompass training and other professional development efforts.